every lie will be the last lie until the next one

john sweet

ISBN: 978-93-6354-995-1

First Edition: 2026
Rs. 200/-

Cyberwit.net
HIG 45 Kaushambi Kunj, Kalindipuram
Allahabad - 211011 (U.P.) India
http://www.cyberwit.net
Tel: +(91) 9415091004
E-mail: info@cyberwit.net

Printed at Repro India Limited.

Contents

i. postcards from the drowning boy

spark/le

find the poet w/ his
tongue nailed to the floor

find his children asleep in
a room filled
with cold sunlight

tell his wife i can show you
the truth but i can't
make you see and she laughs at
how the words twist
in the breeze

she tells you there is never any great
trick to crawling over broken glass

lets you kiss her scars then
tells you you have to leave

tells you life is too short to
waste it always falling in love

wilderness

the sky where it raises
straight up from the hills and
the weight of it and the
sheer enormity

the sun
or not quite

the clouds like shadows of doubt
in the mind of some fading god
and then the flyers i find on
a rest stop bulletin board

a three week-old baby stolen
from a hospital and
missing for seventeen years

and half my life spent
not knowing this

and the sound of passing traffic

the smell of the fields after
three days of rain

my son's tiny hands as he
pulls me
back towards the car

some/one no/where

and this will be the
year i admit defeat

the year of closing doors of
shuttered windows and
why was it exactly
we fell in love?

not every reason matters,
of course

not every war is
fought to be won

look at your father

consider the victims

not their names but the
palaces built on their bones

the tyrants who feast
on their corpses

and maybe ask yourself
what it means to
be human, or don't

either way, you
live you die

you're forgotten

a poem about a
memory and then the
fading memory of
a poem and then
nothing

defeat

admit it

small gift, early autumn

says *i'll make this easy*

says *one plus one* but
insists the answer
be spelled out in blood

dead children on the front lawn

crows

we drove for three hours only to
find the building burned to the
ground when we got there

do you see the punchline?

says she doesn't believe in
god in priests who
refuse to crawl on broken glass

spreads her wings but
never quite takes flight

never quite touches the sun but she
dares you to stand in the space between
hope and desire with only your
faith and a lover who refuses
to speak your name

asks you to give up poetry and
write only prayers

to write them only on the filthy
walls of abandoned churches

says nothing from nothing is both the
past and the future but
she doesn't speak of the present

she doesn't mention any names

without anywhere to go we
can never be lost

the ideal

everything burned and
everyone,
beyond hope,
beyond recognition

sorry

the truth has no shape,
refuses to fit into any
pre-ordained space

the war is won, but no one
can remember why it began

which specific lie was
deemed necessary to rationalize
the first shot,
the first corpse,
the first baby run through
with a bayonet

oh well

cities can be rebuilt
and names forgotten

strangers can write me letters,
tell me i'm an asshole,
a pessimist,

a nihilist,
but what have i done here
besides replay history
without emotion?

who among us didn't believe
that the future of democracy
hung by the thinnest
of threads?

what we finally deserve,
i think,
are the deaths we so
eagerly heap upon others

liberty street collage

some suicide's song on the radio while we
make out on the couch and i
forget your name and you
never speak mine

the last good summer, i think,
or maybe the one after

your sister drunk in the backseat while her
boyfriend goes into the trailer to get the money and
he laughs when she tells him not to get burned

she falls asleep and forgets about the
baby and it won't stop crying

wakes up in the morning
and it's gone

and your father in the hospital or maybe your
mother passed out in the bathroom floor

a near miss?

a pool of blood?

each day the same but
each moment slightly different

each lie less important than the
one that came before

the way we keep waiting for the next one to
be the one that will
finally bring us back to the truth

chain

eight years old and could
never figure out which one of us
did it, but the garage was in flames

the moment was memorized and then
solidified and I grew up hating myself,
which is a different story altogether,
but i can look back now and
see where all true moments intersect

i can love you without fear
and still be afraid

we can swim beneath the surface of
this frozen lake or we can drown

he wakes up to snow, to the news of his father's death

ugly my whole life and
then old on top of it

faith in the absence of faith

hope
but inverted

the age of slaves,
which is eternal,
and then the kingdom of nil

the corpses and the corpse flies and
all of our favorite songs
on the radio

summer 1983,
which i thought would matter

fall 1989
and my first suicide

not much, but all i ever asked
is that you let me be
less than nothing

let me be in love with a future
that has no

we will burn with our own
blinding light there,
you and i

we will nail christ's
trembling hands to the wall
and teach him what it
means to pray

his sugared tears are all
the thanks
we could ever need

sing and burn

this empty nostalgia for the
age of death, for those songs heavy
with bluegrey meaning,
j escariot and g hart both crawling
through their own addictions to
bring flowers to my door

dreams of wide open fields, of
fishscale clouds and sunlight, neverending
tidal shift of freeway traffic, postcards
from the drowning boy

says he'd like to come home but
no one's told him he's dead

no one's told him he's not my
father and so we walk down november
alleyways reading the words of all
the prophets who have been here before us

we watch the execution on tv

contemplate the regrets of
the mothers of tyrants

and what god do you think the
priests paid tribute to as they bulldozed
down the walls of churches filled with refugees?

but no

there is nothing more tiresome
than starving dogs begging for the truth

there is this empty nostalgia for
j christ with his semi-automatic and
his powers of levitation

these oceans filled with the
butchered children of your enemies

the most holy of
wet dreams

in amber

walls of rooms filled w/ dust,
on floors, on hands and knees and blinded

sing w/ your heart

grow scars

this is the place, you see, this house
where the dying man lives, and
there is nothing any of us can do

no blood on the carpet, but a sense
that it could happen at any time

a window

a back yard filled w/ fireflies and twilight

stand there, barefoot, wide-eyed, emotions
carved from dark, sticky wood

speak names softly

breathe in the warmth of
overwhelming joy

stand as still as you can
until all laughter has stopped

and if i could swim

a storm, sleeping

yellow sky and impossible heat

taste of blood when you
spit into the sink

and say this, say
we are not a war and then
smile at your reflection

teeth, outlined in red

faded eyes

in every room, in every corner,
cobwebs, shadows, dust on
pictures of the children

scream of cicadas through
open windows, through warped
& cracked glass

drink the faucet dry

aspirin

codeine

you can't live your whole life
in freefall, and so you grab
onto others

anyone would

everyone does

the illusion of time slowing
down just before you crash

willingly into oblivion

was young and saw the
world as it was

laughed against the pale flesh of
yr stomach
and you asked me what was funny

asked if i'd
remember this moment in ten years
                                        or in twenty

asked like there were lives
depending on it and so i
said *yes*

traced the slow curve of yr breasts
with my free hand and
said *yes*

started waiting for
that day to arrive

poem of obscene wealth

the blood mixed with poison until
i can punch holes through time

yes and then *yes* again and
all kindness offered without shame

all innocence blessed

so easy to make excuses for
pain and for misery

so easy to cause more

fist to rock to blade to gun

gets all screweded up just
like everything else

fear is the engine that drives the
world and whose plan was this?

who invented the need for
gods and prophets?

the need for power and
subservience?

no one with the ability to cause
pain ever truly believes in
justice without punishment

because i will be the dead man of your dreams

and did it help in some small way
when i gave you the truth,
or did your house still burn down wherever you were?

did the distance between us matter?

the death of plath,
        of pilate,
        of cobain,
and the screams of the crows

was it always january?

brown leaves pushing up through
a brittle crust of dirty snow

young boy playing in the frozen mud
down by the river,
there and then gone,
but this is not his song

his name will not be remembered

and don't talk to me about cruelty, okay?

the facts are the facts,
even in this age of liars

i love you and i love you and what is time
but a weapon used against us?

and the act of giving feels wrong here

feels too much like the act of losing,
like the fine art of getting lost in empty spaces

i was a fool for growing old,
for digging in and
will i call 500,000 miles of running in
steadily diminishing circles
a life?

yes, but i've begun
to doubt myself

i've begun to understand the need for oblivion
and for personal annihilation

always felt good kneeling at your feet

always felt pure kissing the filth
from your eyes, and so what now?

the truth,
but maybe the truth changes

maybe you hit the wall too hard

the drugs aren't enough or your child became a burden or
the snow followed you wherever you tried to hide

the ice got into your veins,
the frost filled your heart, or maybe all of
this imagery is just a simple blanket of denial

maybe we both became less

maybe there is a hole in the world
where all of the light runs out

what is there left to look for in
the dark but comfort?

mirage

drugstore at the
farthest edge of the desert but
we had a map,
had my hands in your blood,
had your teeth in my heart and
this was the new world

august and then september and
all of de chirico's promises come true
and we thought about offering
christ a blindfold
but why?

better to see the bullet

better to just put on your best
leather boots and walk the 3000
miles to your father's grave

get down on your knees among
his bleached and broken
bones and sing

flight

no time to die
and no need

eighty miles an hour down
an empty highway in the
early autumn sunlight

close yr eyes

breathe

don't talk about pain with the
people you love,
and don't talk about god

let the bodies stay
nailed to their crosses

let the exit you choose
be the one that
arrives at the ocean

step out into the
luminous air and run

a wasted mouthful

nothing to lead and nowhere to
go and no one
cares if you die anyway

no one cares if you
live in sight of the land

we are all kingdoms, right?

we all go to sleep

we all burn

and don't apologize, but don't
expect any applause, either

the best gifts
remain unspoken

the best years are always
referred to in the past tense

do you see how that's funny?

do you understand the
alchemy
of corpse into god?

talk to cobain about
his cure for addiction

ask if he sees the irony in
the voice of a generation
being a suicide

once you've got that
sense of humor, there's really
nothing else you need

ii. the only way to arrive at the future

if you should speak...

a good trick, disappearing,
but only if you tell nobody

only if the hills
remain the hills, the sky
blue

a perfect afternoon,
but late in the season and
the boat has gone missing

the tracks turn to memory at
the desert's edge

and what to do with these
false kings but let them
drown in the cesspools of
their own petty hatreds?

where to point the gun but
into the crowd?

a true believer only accepts
their own immortality
until the blood begins to flow

every act of faith is an
empty gesture when seen

in the pale light of
september afternoons

why the hell would you
offer me god when all i
ever wanted was
the truth?

the infinite

a waste of words,

i love you or *i hate you*
while the days crawl away from
us like wounded animals

five years then ten then twenty and
what are you doing
still looking for deeper meaning?

de chirico said it all by leaving
everything important unsaid

cobain took matters into his own hands
and what a joke without a punchline that was,
but it's blood the children want

it's the illusion of
death as sacrifice

a hole in the heart
where all light pours out and if i
can't come to grips with my own death
i can at least learn to accept yours

i can try to make you smile but i
can never figure out
how to get you to stop crying

have we reached the
center of the labyrinth yet?

there's god and there's the truth but
you can't have both

there's late afternoon sunlight and
the shadows cast
by everything it falls on

a waste of time placing
monetary value on human endeavors
but this is what we do

this is why we fail

wake up one day as dead as
anyone's savior and
all that's left for the rest of us is
to forget you

says *tell me something i don't know;* tells me to keep it to myself

or that our pasts have
no meaning, no
value

assassinate the president,
butcher the pregnant women, it all
just ends up on a t-shirt
sooner or later

becomes a catchphrase, maybe,
or a meme, or some obscure pop culture
reference played for laughs

an argument for the
end of the human race

seems like there's always
room for just one more

a slow fire

i tell you it's music,
is a thing alive,
and you ask if it will burn

september,
blinding light but fading heat,
and i've found you here,
or you've found me,
or we've discovered each other

a touch, a kiss,
a moment opening up like a flower

words, yes, but cautiously

there is still the fear of
spilling whatever it is we hold

there is still the fear of
hurting you

of losing the gifts
you've given me

consider all of the doors we've
closed
just to reach this day

or the plague years, which were foretold

dead man in a dead man's car, which means
one of us must be a liar, but i
know it's not me and i would never blame you

i would move to the city,
but the cities are doomed

the dogs are hungry

they will never grow fat on the truth,
will never grow old in this age of disease,
and it's one thing to believe all those lies, and then it's
something else altogether to invent them

it's the language of thieves
and of whores

100,000 years of self-induced famine, and
i sleep without dreaming before
waking up in a stranger's bed

i give my children names that they reject

i give them what i think is love,
but they grow up afraid

they grow up american

they learn to wear their
mindless hatred with empty pride

[we've been here for too long; not long enough]

or these silent moments of despair,
which always end up lasting our entire lives

your father's addictions

your grandfather's suicide
and all pain leads to humor, yes,
but maybe not soon enough

all houses burn down at their own speed

the baby is saved but the mother disappears
and then the year of the plague arrives,
and what point is there in praying to a god who doesn't
give a shit whether you live or die?

what point is there to a
king in any form?

we all become the enemies of
whoever wields the power
when we have none to call our own

in praise.

in the grey in the
snow the wounded animal in
first light and he is not dead he is
just breathing / he is just in
the back yard in the dirty snow in the
grey in the week after his
51st birthday / not lost but
afraid not wounded but dying in
the almost snow in the almost
light and out behind the
garage and he is the animal and
fear is what he believes

the fear he believes

the grey

the later years, in which
all of this is forgotten but
for now,
now

the moment which is here and
the one he has lost and
he is not the animal he is
what comes before
and after

he is not the grey

not frightened
but afraid

not wounded
but dying

the bitter god that is
born from the
ruins of the animal

[what a suffocating place to be]

or depression like a
tv screen
filled with static

like the sky seen
from below
the ocean's surface

no point trying to
write it all down
until you can
at least figure out
how to swim

[i think we all misheard]

and my brother in one room and
my sister on the floor and
all of us liars

all of us dying
our entire lives

small fingers scratching at the
kitchen door,
but nothing to be afraid of

but nothing

and not a whole lot of time,
but what were you expecting?

after the war comes the plague and
then, after the plague, a war

man across the street with a gun,
and this is what his
youngest child shoots him with

irony, maybe,
if that's your thing,
or maybe tragedy

maybe vengeance

we all need to figure out
exactly how much shit we're
willing to eat, then plan
our next move

consider who we love

measure the distance from
this desert to the next

understand that you will only
ever be a reflection of
whatever emptiness you embrace

the surrealist in exile

and it was that last good summer or
maybe the one before it,
no wife no
mortgage no wars call our own and when i
found you was it me you were crying for?

were we awake
when the storm passed through?

rumors of snow
even on the warmest days and so we laughed

tried to explain the joke to paalen but
he couldn't hear us with the gun to his head

the boy was wrapped in too many layers of
sunlight to drown, but he did

the paintings were sold and the
books burned and
it was some 13 year-old kid down in arizona
who smiled into the camera and said it
was time for all the jews to
go back where they came from

it was the idea of america as an abject failure

that last good summer
grown cold without warning

children drowning in the blood of
other children and all you
could do was tell me that it wasn't funny

all we could do was laugh

the omnipresent blues

between the desert and the
certainty of the desert
you were saying *that*
can’t be true

you were in love with the idea
of being more than your
mother’s hatred

were drunk on the
knowledge that i didn’t know
everything and,
when we spoke, our
words were thick with blood

when you left, i had
nothing to write about
but myself

finally understood
what an asshole i was

between defeat and despair

first week of april all brown lawns and
grey sky, threat of snow that
never quite arrives and
what i miss are
leonora's pale breasts in the mexican sunlight

do you remember 1937?

are we still killing for the
same reasons we were then?

seems like it was all pretty funny until
we realized that everyone
who'd died was someone we'd known

and everyone talks about dying, always

house on fire for 20 years now, and
that the kids never call anymore

that the drugs don't work

think you're high, but mostly
you're just depressed

mostly you're just bleeding

and it feels good, sure,
but it's the law of diminishing returns

it's the idea that hope matters,
but that it
still saves no one in the end

the setup and the punchline
all rolled into one

a fist squeezed too tight to
ever hold anything but pain

don't tell me it's not funny
just because it's your own

[in spaceship days, when you and i were young]

always the same story, says he
was drunk up in the cockpit but not as
drunk as the bombardier, says it was raining blood and
the goddamn kid wouldn't stop
screaming

says he knew the war was finally over
because everyone here was dead

says there was nothing to do now but
catch the next bus home and
fall in love

wait for the news that the
last politician had been hung

YESNO

she says *no pity for the*
failed magicians, says *no*
mercy for the priests or the
politicians

says *make every shot count* and
she laughs at her
brother found hanging in the shower

weeps bitter tears at the idea of
christ's return

smiles when she kisses me
and then she leaves for good

[trapped in a cage and surrendered too soon]

kid overdoses on
mandies after the show,
gets dumped in a tub of ice water,
drowns,
and so he misses the punchline

he misses the part where
everyone laughs

misses the rest of the
whole goddamn century

suicide days (1)

season of dead waitresses,
of endless sunshine and baggie after
baggie of sammy's best weed

eight fifty an hour and
mary in the back room on her
fifteen minute break, up against the
wall and calling me by her
boyfriend's name

nikki in the parking lot,
giving me back the picture of
her i'd done in watercolors
and pastel

gets back in the car with
her boyfriend and he
gives me the finger, peels out,
and i toss the painting
in the dumpster

i go back inside and ask
shelley for a ride home

start waiting for the day when
all of this shit
might begin to seem funny

iii. there is only the present and there is only the bitter past

walk away/like a fool

someone telling you *it's*
almost too late your entire life,
and then it is, and is this
comedy or is it
tragedy?

do you outlive your children or
bury them all one at a time?

and maybe i'm part of
this particular picture

maybe the sunlight is
never as pure as we remember

you're smiling at the edge of
a field of flowers, but
there are always shadows
spilling across your face

there are always angry
voices reach in from
other rooms

blame to be assigned and
refused and
some of us grow up while
others just grow old

some of us grow wings

none of us escape

what you feel about this
never really makes
any difference in the end

my last year as a landscape painter

cemetery at the end of tracy
st waiting for snow or
rain or the news of war

down to the river

empire of bald tires and
rusted grocery carts

sound of the interstate

sudden sunlight through a
small break in the clouds, but
don't turn it into something
more than it actually is

[when we're lovers at last]

The wide-open space of sunlit afternoons,
and the fear. Man at the edge of the freeway
asks if you believe in god, and then steps
into northbound traffic. Sunday. Monday,
Call in sick. Drive to the house where
your mother watched your father die.
Drive past it.
Fifty more miles to the south shore of
Cayuga Lake, and are you happy yet?
Do you feel anything at all?
Listen;
I'm not going to spend the rest of my life
apologizing for your pain. I'm not going to
pretend we ever had a chance. You start off
with the small lies but, still, the world's
gone up in flames by the end.

small gift, early autumn

says *i'll make this easy*

says *one plus one* but
insists the answer
be spelled out in blood

dead children on the front lawn

crows

we drove for three hours only to
find the building burned to the
ground when we got there

do you see the punchline?

says she doesn't believe in
god in priests who
refuse to crawl on broken glass

spreads her wings but
never quite takes flight

never quite touches the sun but she
dares you to stand in the space between
hope and desire with only your
faith and a lover who refuses
to speak your name

asks you to give up poetry and
write only prayers

to write them only on the filthy
walls of abandoned churches

says nothing from nothing is both the
past and the future but
she doesn't speak of the present

she doesn't mention any names

without anywhere to go we
can never be lost

[from the time we were young]

august light and
september air

ask de chirico

we have always been in love,
                                        you and i,
but we have always been lost

all clocks stopped

all moments equal
and unfaded

undiminished

and i am tired of being 24
                              of being 37
                              of being 52

i am tired of living in
a desert of my own creation

give me someone to
blame for my mistakes and
i will only be the same
as everyone else

topanga canyon postcard

ex-lover crawls to california,
writes him letters in holy blood

tells him there is only the
present and there is only the bitter past

do you see?

blue sky after
two weeks of rain

the subtle joy of laughing into
the face of certain mortality

deaths of parents
          of children
          of enemies and friends and then
the subtle pleasure of a dreamed escape

and think about breathing in
this age of poison

the possibility of mercy
                              maybe
or the absolute absence of sin

no end to hunger

no end to despair

no end to pain, finally,
and she tells him she loves him
                    only to
find out that it could never be enough

could never fill the hole she's been
digging for the past 40 years

100,000,000 minor deaths in the age of forgetting

last days of july among the weeds and dying flowers
in some anonymous back yard,
some forgotten rust-belt town,
and i am standing here casting the shadow of my father's ghost

i am helping the junkies overdose,
but it's a waste of energy digging graves

let the bodies be piled in the ragweed fields
out beyond the abandoned factories

let them bloat beneath the silver sun,
let them split wide open to feed the vultures,
the crows,
the true believers

let the prophets of a more compassionate future
truly have the gift of vision

palais

not the artist but
the artist's lover

the dead man found
on the bathroom floor

tell him he's gonna
be famous, but all
he does is cry

Allegory w/ sunlight & clouds

i want to give him a name,
this man with the head of a crow,
but he has none

i want to give him a purpose

a city, maybe, to call his own,
but he stands there at the edge of
a field, holding the bones of
someone's child

stands there.
naked and smeared with dirt

with blood

understands that the
american century has finally
arrived

[everything i gave is what i need]

she says she's sorry
she hates

says she's sorry
i'm dead,
and why would she lie?

this is love

every second counts,
right?

all versions of the future
end up guttering out
in the past

all cities collapse
beneath the weight of
their own poverty

and she says
she's sorry,
and she is, and i
tell her she's
beautiful

i tell her this is love

she tells me she’s
sorry we’re dead

i think i believe her

because we are only dimming light

Kid tells you *please never die*, and you
have no answer. And it's true that one of you
doesn't deserve the other. It's true that every
ugly suicide is just one more domino falling
to help bring us closer to endgame.
Remember? Shani in the summer of drugs,
and then her father, and then Chris, and all
you wanted at fifteen was to get laid, and at
20 and at 25, and then by 30 you just wanted
to lock the door and hide in a darkened room.
Just wanted to keep the shades pulled and
your eyes closed. Wait for the future to
finally mean as much as the past.

love poem in the kingdom of blind dogs

and i thought we trusted
each other, or i thought we
believed each other

i thought the knife
would go in cleanly

that the pain
would be tolerable

six years spent driving down the
same goddamn roads every day
but you'd disappeared

left me stoned at the edge of some
ocean i'd never seen before

lost behind anonymous doors in
faceless neighborhoods and i
woke up dead on
the morning of the funeral

maybe a couple of drinks

maybe a handful of pills, and
strange that the sky
could be so blue

strange that i remembered you
as sunlight

as oxygen

and you in the hallway, laughing,
saying *now isn't the time to*
fall in love and then
twenty years later,
then thirty-five

my life as a cage and my
country as a wasteland and
you and i invisible against
the slowly fading landscape

you and i
without end

menace

and there is always danger in
leaving a trail, in leaving
proof of your past lives

denial becomes an artform,
lies become oxygen

do you practice in
front of mirrors?

on your children?

you are always more or
less than what you seem

for myself, and for you

where the wind makes more wind or where
the children sleep inside their dreams, where the
cop walks backwards and blind, the wrong door,
the wrong time, shoots a stranger in a stranger's house and
it's a joke, a riddle, a puzzle, two trains moving in
opposite directions at different speeds and i listen to
the slowing sound of my breathing, i lie next to this
woman who used to be my lover, the two us no
longer near the center of the universe, an approximate
lifetime of pulling away, of empty words, mouths
filled with clay, hands bound, hearts turned inward,
and i'm afraid here and i'm lost and i'm afraid

time, in all directions

or the minor acts of dead men

of forgotten lovers

you live in the past
                    present
                  or future
and make no apologies

am i inventing you
correctly here?

fifteen wasted years and
then five good ones
and then the cancer

the phone call from his sister on a
weekend i was out of town and
what if i tell her the joke but
forget the punchline?

there are other lives at stake here,
you understand

gods taking bullets and
newborn babies set on fire and
all of the pits being dug by
anonymous soldiers on the
edges of factory towns

all of the wars that are started
while we sleep

all of the letters from home
that get lost along the way

never knew you were loved
until it was
too late to matter

kiss me in the autumn sunlight

and i'll tell you
i'm an asshole
and you'll laugh

seems simple enough
but nothing ever is

nothing ever was

the past into the
future, right?

we could do it
blindfolded

we could hold
hands and jump

it's only a long way
down if you look

[all i know is that nothing has changed]

a minor poet in a world of
minor poets, but the important thing is
that everyone dies

the important thing is that
everyone is eventually
forgotten

iv. a nail through the tongue or a spike through the heart

[one foot free, one foot caught]

a blind man painting
the face of god

a fist

flesh and bone and
bottomless blue sky, and
what exactly are we getting at here?

sex and depression,
probably,
and sometimes together

sometimes the wrong pills

a song on the radio carrying
too much weight and
we are always moving towards the future and
we are always being dragged down
                                        by the past

we are always sleeping with
the wrong ghosts

i am never sorry enough
for the pain i cause

it always arrives with
the promise of more

unnamed angel

these people who love you and
you a stranger among them,
a war in a ruined city,
a god without the possibility of ever
becoming anything more

you with your sense of loss
      with your desire for escape

an open window at midnight
and the distant sound of freeway traffic

father's ghost in the bedroom doorway
head wreathed in flames &
carrion stench

not a dream he tells you
but in someone else's voice and then
it's your youngest son crying out
in his sleep, screaming in terror,
but you can't find his room

you can't see the shore

daybreak, both hands
cut off at the wrist and so how
do you stay afloat?

what do you drink in
this ocean of dust?

too many questions with
no obvious answers

too many effortless ways in
which beauty can be
destroyed

this is the basis
for all of history

birthday song

inherit the failure gene
  the self-loathing gene
          the suicide gene
but then try not to
pass them on

go ahead

i dare you

golgotha postcard

pilate shot through the throat and
then the crows at his heart

the dogs drinking his tears

grow up fast or
not at all,
right?

a lifetime of dying played out in
the space of an hour and i
forget if i ever told you i loved you that summer

i forget if you were the one who
taught me how to bleed

was too busy making promises that
turned without effort into
such heartfelt lies

[i'm staying right here; i won't move til i'm dead]

all these houses growing up,
some in the suburbs,
some on the sides of mountains,
and never any sidewalks

it fucks you up somehow

makes you sleep with the
younger sisters of
guys you barely know

makes you remember
crap that never happened,
or at least that's what your mother tells you,
but she's pushing 80 by this point

says the babysitter never
got you high when you were seven,
says you were never left at a bar while your
father drove a few towns over to
help his buddy fix a car, but
you remember the way the waitress
smiled whenever she brought you
another coke

you remember the way she smelled
and the color of her hair,
but you have no memories of
your father coming back

seems like he must have,
though,
because here you are,
and your mother tells you
you're full of shit

tells you
you whined a lot,
read too many books,
stole money from her purse when
you thought she was in a
different part of the house

tells you she knew your
first wife was a mistake, says she
figured out your second would
be a suicide eight months
before it happened, and
what you have now
is this house with a sidewalk

the empty rooms your
children no longer live in,
and you think they might
still love you

you think there might
still be possibilities you
haven't even considered

it's a terrifying
way to live

innocence

shadows of birds enormous
over the sides of houses

not silence, but oblivion

sound of traffic, of sirens,
drowned out by small fears
and obvious truths

blue sky and sunlight held
together with simple magic,
and what about rothko lying
dead from simultaneous
attempts at suicide?

what about the invisible
sacred strings that tie you to
all of the things you
love most in life?

listen

in the end, we are all just
starving dogs in the eyes of
someone else's god

in the end, desire is just
another form of hunger

i would tell you how
often i think about you
just to see your smile

i would lie, but never
without noble intentions

never without one hand
reaching out in fear

permafrost

was suddenly mortal in the
cold blue sunlight of my 35th winter

was lost in a motel room w/ a stranger and
her sister and both of them naked
and one of them crying and we
were far beyond the point where
words would help explain anything

i was considering rothko,
wrists slashed and overdosed on
his kitchen floor

i was considering his daughter

the ease with which pain
spreads out from the core

in the palace of empty promises

fear of dying vs. the fear of
living yr whole life
never even knowing you were dead

right?

fear of waking up on the
last day and realizing you never did
anything worth remembering
                                        at all

bread, meat

sky like no sky,
late winter,
all objects without shadows

all shadows
deep underground

walk further north to where
the totems no longer
hold magic

stand to one side and
watch the babies starve

watch the mothers try to
keep them alive with religion

hatred is easy

it's the trick of aiming
that takes time

to kill your own kind
is a mercy, to kill those
above you a crime

consider who it was
that made these rules

cut them open to see
what makes them tick

put the pieces back
together in a better way

naming the ghost: a softer dirge

one of us bleeding, yes,
but none of us whole and
you tell me you're sorry

you lock the doors while rain
comes in through all
the open windows and we
laugh without joy at the
pain we cause each other

at the sorrow of the stars

and what about your lover
who chooses wealth over happiness?

what about your husband who
can't stop inventing
reasons to leave?

both of the bleeding, yes,
and both of them
bound to the future

a nail through the tongue or
a spike through the heart

some bitter scrap of poem left
behind by a poet who
died before he could finish it

not a map but
a darkened room

a clenched fist
punching a brick wall

your pain can only matter
if it's the source
of someone else's joy

demonology

the drowning man is
not a religion

this much i know

the weight of god is not a gift,
and so we buy each other guns instead

we let the starving starve,
but we tell them we care

we make movies about their deaths,
we build our cities from their bones

say *good morning* and say
  good morning and say
  good night and if
the passing days lack meaning

if the false kings agree
to die for our sins

let it be called a victory and
let my hands know
nothing but the warmth of your bare flesh

let each day be the day before
your father's suicide

it's possible still that he
might change his mind

this country of polished chrome, these ancient ruins

made a flag from the bones
of dead soldiers, built a nation from
the skins of the natives

raped children in full sight of god

in houses of prayer
in houses of shame where the
water ran black

where the dogs ate what the
priests puked up
and we hid in alleyways
and we started fires where the
homeless slept

we were the bitter
hands of jesus

we had come to stone
his lover

she said pain was better
than feeling nothing at all

[it's just me; i can't deny]

this almost silence, this
late october sunlight, straight-up blue sky
and all the neighbors smoking pot,
sitting at their windows watching me
sit in my back yard, ragged lawn,
dying trees, run-down house
and this is it

this is the sum total of 57 years,
and i don't think i'm dying of
any one particular thing,
but i'm dying

we all are

and the garage slowly rots,
slowly collapses,
slowly burns,
and the last of the bees hover
sluggishly in the eaves

two late-season rose-blooms
and a hydrangea,
phlox,
ivy,
the hastas with their pitted leaves,
and i remember being born into
one war and then being

too old for the next, or at
least too indifferent

i remember thinking i owed my country
nothing more than i was
already giving it,
and that hasn't changed

i think i'm still
who i thought i was

i think i still understand
what the truth is

think maybe i think about
suicide too much,
even here,
even in the sunlight,
some asshole coming down jackson ave too fast,
a woman shouting at him and
then he's gone

then it's just the shadows of trees
etched up the sides of houses,
the shadows of houses cut deep into earth
and the stealthy creep of weeds,
of strangling vines and
choking ground cover, and
who the fuck actually believes in
the power of art when we're caught
beneath this neverending crush of

taxes, heating bills, mortgages,
dental check-ups and car insurance?

what have we given up to
acquire this particular here and now?

and still, here i am,
older than i was twenty minutes ago,
thinking about the prescription my doctor
never called in to the pharmacy,
breathing in the smell of
pot and gasoline

here i am,
knowing the day is coming

knowing winter,
or the thought of winter,
or the absolute weight of it,
will be what kills me and,
if not that,
then spring or fall or the devastating
sorrow that comes with summer

the almost silence of
this overgrown back yard

this is it

[kill the pain but dull the joy]

a small motion,
a finger on the trigger, a
pilot light or a vacuum cleaner hose

a moment
and then the moment after

the bones of newborns
ground beneath bootheels

will we call it victory?

will our speeches be forgotten?

progress, we'll say, which is
always defined by the deaths of others

my house, which is
no longer a home

my children, who understand
the failure i've become

unconditional love, yes,
but for how long?

i have been a rock
but will become an anchor

picture your life as
a bottomless ocean

50, 60 years of treading water,
and then what?

the fine art of
drifting away from shore

all strength given way
to hopelessness

a small motion,
a shrug or a flinch

a beautiful summer day,
but the windows have been painted over,
the door locked from the other side,
and so consider everything you've
come to fear multiplied by
100,000

consider the inevitability of
a war fought in vain

a small moment towards the end
and then the moment after

corpses and vultures

the emptiness of faith

and will you turn to me in these
last sunlit days of our youth and say
time means nothing?

will you make me believe,
or at least make me love you?

shouldn't be hard

i have these memories of
some other future

a small fleeting moment where
either of us could be anyone

you, silhouetted against a
pale copper sky, laughing at me
at the water's edge and
listen

every act creates a ripple

each beginning moves us
closer to the end

a small motion, a finger on
a trigger or a hand
reaching out in comfort

a moment and
then a moment lost

the clarity that comes with
a headful of poison

we are all of us immortal
right up until
the moment we die

tell you a secret, tell you a lie

so dig deeper into freedom,
into the idea of god vs.
no god

eat yr weight in
sorrow & misery

spend all yr useless afternoons in the
bedrooms of welfare mothers
getting high, and do you remember
where you were when the
president was shot?

or maybe the fact of his death is
really all that matters

morrison, lennon, christ, cobain,
they'll all be
forgotten in time, too

this is not the age of saints
you understand

we are not the ghosts
of greater or lesser men

the planes come in low,
the bombs are dropped and
all we're taught to sing

are songs of freedom

all we're given to drink is
the blood of our enemy

a goddamn bitter taste but it
always
leaves us thirsty for more

www.ingramcontent.com/pod-product-compliance
Ingram Content Group UK Ltd.
Pitfield, Milton Keynes, MK11 3LW, UK
UKHW041315190726
13845UKWH00025B/276

9 789363 549951